MY LIFE

My Behavior

WRITTEN BY C.J. POLIN
ILLUSTRATED BY RYAN WHEATCROFT

PowerKiDS press
New York

Published in 2023 by The Rosen Publishing Group, Inc.
29 East 21st Street, New York, NY 10010

Editors: Sarah Peutrill and Sarah Ridley
Design: Anthony Hannant (Little Red Ant)

Cataloging-in-Publication Data

Names: Polin, C.J. | Wheatcroft, Ryan, illustrator.
Title: My behavior / by C.J. Polin, illustrated by Ryan Wheatcroft.
Description: New York : Powerkids Press, 2023. | Series: My life | Includes glossary and index.
Identifiers: ISBN 9781725338098 (pbk.) | ISBN 9781725338111 (library bound) | ISBN 9781725338104 (6pack) | ISBN 9781725338128 (ebook)
Subjects: LCSH: Social psychology--Juvenile literature. | Human behavior--Juvenile literature. | Intergroup relations--Juvenile literature. | Social ethics--Juvenile literature.
Classification: LCC HM1035.P655 2023 | DDC 305--dc23

Manufactured in the United States of America

CPSIA Compliance Information: Batch #CSPK23. For further information contact Rosen Publishing, New York, New York at 1-800-237-9932.

Find us on

CONTENTS

WHAT IS BEHAVIOR?

Behavior is the way you act. You might change your behavior depending on who you are with and where you are. For example, loud shouting is usually fine for the playground, but it is bad behavior for the classroom.

It's okay to run around and be noisy in the playground ...

Good Behavior

Do you like people to be nice to you? Most of us would say, "Yes!" So you should behave in a nice way to other people. Being nice can mean lots of different things, but it always includes being kind to the people around you. It may also include being polite, clean, and tidy.

When you behave well, it means that you and everyone around you gets along better and has more fun.

?

Do you change the way you act with different people and in different places? How?

... but in the classroom, it's usually best to stay seated and listen carefully.

Bad Behavior

We call some bad behavior "bad manners," such as picking your nose in front of people, talking with your mouth full, or sticking out your tongue. Being rude or hurtful to other people or doing anything that puts yourself or others in danger is also bad behavior.

BEHAVIOR AND FEELINGS

Have you noticed that behavior and feelings are connected? Your feelings affect your actions, and your actions affect your feelings. Good behavior makes other people feel good about you. Then you feel good about yourself.

How Others Behave

Think about how the behavior of other people makes you feel. How do you feel if someone calls you nasty names? You probably don't feel very happy. But if someone helps you with your work or invites you to join their game, you feel happy.

When Bethany bumped into Jason in the park, she asked him whether he'd like to hang out with her for a bit. They both had fun and felt happy.

Bad Mood Blues

We can't feel happy all the time. It's normal to feel all sorts of emotions. Sometimes you might feel angry or grumpy and not in the mood to behave well. What could you do to make yourself feel better?

You could talk to someone or take some time on your own to calm down. If you make that huge effort to behave better, you might find that you feel a lot better too.

?

Who can you talk to when you're in a bad mood?

Jaina was in a bad mood and spilled water over his painting. Now she feels bad for upsetting him and says sorry. Both of them feel better.

MAGIC WORDS

Good behavior begins with a few small words that are very special. Using these words shows that you are polite. Being polite means that you are not bossy and that you appreciate people's help or kindness.

Please

Add this magic word whenever you ask for something. "Please will you help me?" "May I please have a pencil?" It's the nice way to ask for something.

Thank You

When someone does something nice for you, thank them. If someone opens the door for you, gives you a present, or lets you have a turn on the swing, remember to say "thank you." It shows that you are grateful for their kindness.

Mia and Harry remember to say "please" and "thank you" to the school lunch helper. That makes the lunch helper smile.

Excuse Me

Say "excuse me" or "sorry" when you need to get someone's attention, when you bump into someone, or when you need to get through a crowd. When you yawn, burp, or fart in front of someone you can also say "excuse me."

I'm Sorry

It's often hard to say you're sorry. It means admitting that you've done something wrong. But people think more of you if you are willing to admit your mistakes, whether you've accidentally stepped on someone's toe or you've had an argument with a friend.

?

How does it make you feel when people say the magic words to you? How about when people don't say the magic words?

A REASON FOR RULES

Why do we need rules? Imagine trying to play a game without any rules. Everyone would play the game a different way. There would be lots of confusion and probably arguments too. Rules let everyone know how to behave so that we can all work and play together in a way that keeps us happy and safe.

Nadia and her friends have fun playing together because they know the rules and don't care too much about who wins.

School Rules

Many schools have a list of rules. These are often posted around the building to help you remember them. These rules are usually about safety and good behavior. Everyone at the school must follow exactly the same rules so we all stay safe.

Here are some school rules. What are the rules at your school?

SCHOOL RULES

- We will try hard.
- We will follow instructions.
- We will raise our hands in class.
- We will be kind to others.
- We will keep the school tidy.

?

Why is raising hands in class a good school rule?

Following Instructions

Does your teacher tell you to walk quietly in the halls? Do your parents ask you to hurry and get ready for school? You might not like instructions such as these, but they help get things done safely and quickly.

WITH FRIENDS

Friends are fun to be with, but even more important, good friends are kind to each other. With them, there's no need to do something you don't want to do or behave in a way that you don't think is right just to fit in. Good friends like you the way you are.

Making New Friends

You may have a group of best friends, but try to include other children as well so that no one is left out. If someone seems shy or lonely, be friendly. Ask that person to join you and introduce him or her to your friends. It's not only a nice thing to do, but you may also find that the new person becomes a great new friend.

Imagine being new to a school and not knowing anyone. What would you want the other children to do?

Jaden doesn't know Tom very well, but he invites him to sit with his friends so that Tom isn't left out.

Playing and Sharing

How do you feel when you don't get a turn at a game or with a particular toy? You think it's not fair, don't you? So always play fairly: take turns and share with others. Be a good sport too. This means don't cheat and be nice to the winners even if you're disappointed that you've lost.

Even though Kelly's team lost the game, they still congratulate the winners. Perhaps they'll be the winners next time.

AT HOME

When you're at home, you probably just want to relax and be yourself—and that's a good thing. But you share your home with other people, so you do need to think about them as well.

Brothers and Sisters

If you have brothers and sisters, you probably find that sometimes you're the best of friends and other times you fight. It's hard to get along all the time. But taking turns and sharing is just as important with family as it is with friends.

Ella is annoyed because her brother Ari won't let her get on the trampoline with him or take turns.

Try to sort out small disagreements before they become big problems.

Getting Along

Sometimes when you're in a bad mood, you might behave badly toward your family. But that's not fair. If you are in a bad mood, try talking about your feelings with your parent or caregiver before you start shouting! And don't be too proud to say sorry if you have hurt someone's feelings.

?

What changes can you make to your behavior to help you get along better with your family?

Rules at Home

You'll have rules at home to follow too. Sometimes you might have to help with the chores. You can help your parents or caregivers by being tidy and doing the chores they ask you to. It may be boring, but if everyone helps out, the jobs get done quicker.

It's Heidi's job to help Dad tidy up the kitchen after dinner. They make a good team.

OUT AND ABOUT

When you're out and about, you want to stay safe, so you've got to think harder about your behavior and keep out of danger. You also need to care for the outdoor spaces you visit.

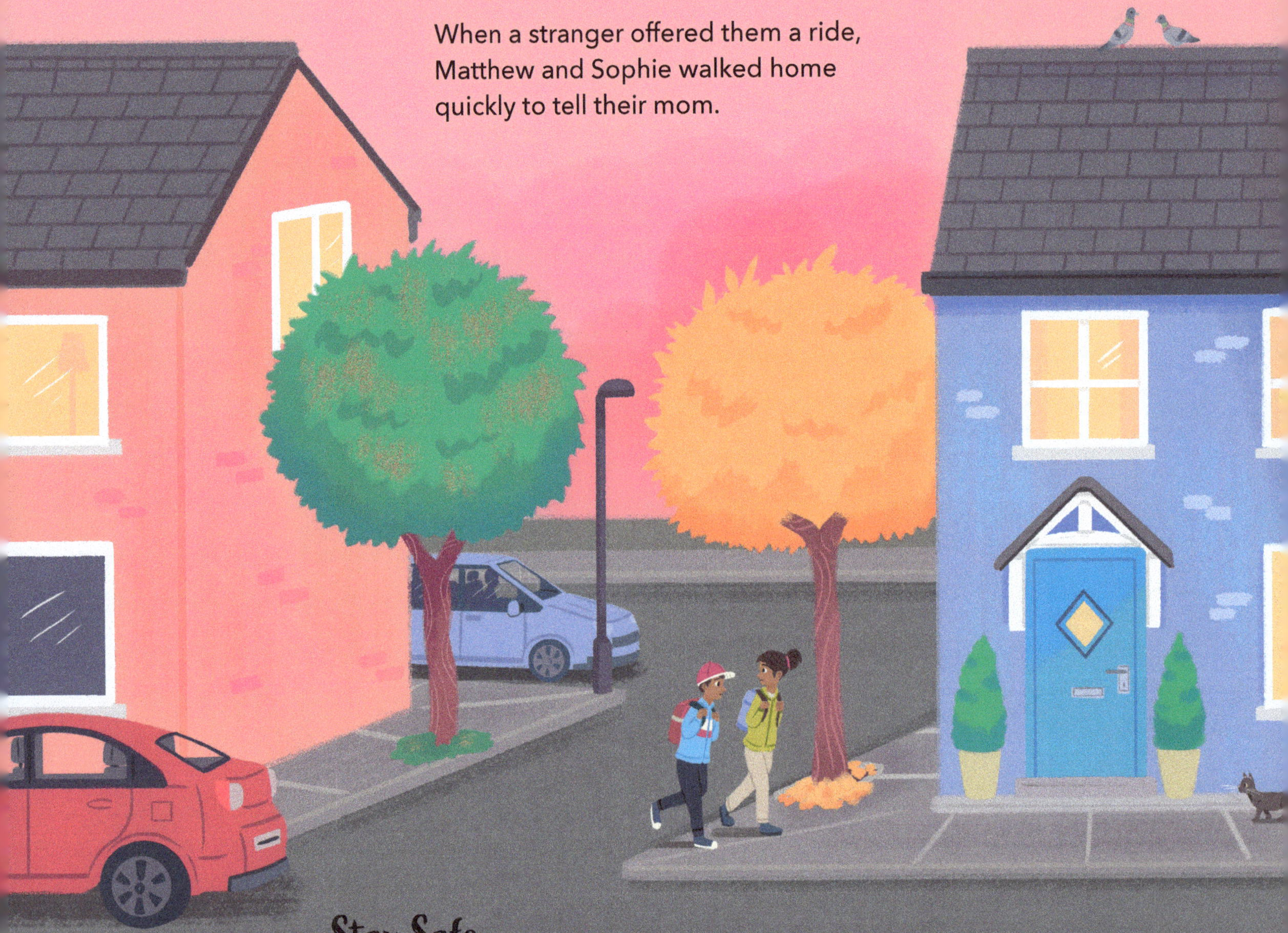

When a stranger offered them a ride, Matthew and Sophie walked home quickly to tell their mom.

Stay Safe

Make sure your parents or caregivers always know where you are. If you run off without telling anyone, you could get lost. Never go anywhere with people you don't know.

Road Safety

Roads can be dangerous places, so be careful and walk on safe paths or sidewalks. Only cross the road at safe places, such as pedestrian crossings, and remember to look both ways for traffic on the road. Wear bright clothes or reflectors so you can be seen in the dark, and always wear a safety helmet when you ride your bike or scooter.

Luke and Jessie always look both ways before they cross the road.

Be Green!

Don't be a litter bug–hold on to your trash until you find a garbage can to put it in. Take home other trash to recycle it. Always treat plants, green spaces, and wild areas with respect and care.

BE PATIENT

Being patient can be hard. But if everyone wanted everything right this minute, there would be a lot of bad tempers. Being patient shows that you are thinking of other people.

?

What can you do to help time pass more quickly when you are waiting?

Leo doesn't like being at the back of the line, but he knows he must wait his turn.

Waiting

It may seem like you're always waiting for something–waiting in lines; waiting for your teacher to choose you; waiting for your mom or dad to take you out; or waiting for your turn on the swing. Waiting is not easy, but be patient and your turn will come. No one likes waiting, but it does mean everyone gets a fair turn.

Jody interrupts her mom on the telephone, but her mom gives her a sign to wait until she's finished.

Don't Interrupt

When someone is speaking, be patient and wait until the person is finished before you speak. This is also important if someone is speaking on the phone. Only interrupt if there is an emergency.

DON'T BE RUDE

When you behave rudely, you show that you don't care how the people around you feel. Isn't it better to be polite so that people enjoy being with you?

Disgusting Behavior

Try not to burp or fart in front of other people, and certainly don't pick your nose! There's no point trying to use disgusting behavior to show off. It doesn't work. You might think this sort of behavior is funny, but it isn't at all nice for the people around you.

Don't Spread Germs

Germs make people ill. Stop germs from spreading by covering your mouth when you cough and your nose when you sneeze. Use a tissue to catch sneezes, blow your nose, or wipe a drippy nose. When you are finished with the tissue, put it in a garbage can and wash your hands as soon as you can. Wash your hands after you have been to the bathroom and before you have anything to eat.

Ah-choo! Ryan quickly catches his sneeze in a tissue.

Table Manners

Table manners aren't hard to learn. You get to practice them three times a day!

?

Why do you think table manners are important?

Emily uses table manners at school, at home, and anywhere she eats.

Here's a reminder of how to eat politely:

- Stay in your seat. If you must get up, say "excuse me."
- Use your fork, knife, and spoon to eat, not your hands (unless it's a sandwich or other finger food).
- Wipe sticky fingers or a messy mouth on a napkin, not on your clothes.
- Eat with your mouth closed.
- Remember to use your magic words when you ask for or are given something.

NASTY BEHAVIOR

Nasty behavior hurts people. Hitting, kicking, punching, or pinching is NOT okay. Lying, stealing, or cheating isn't either. You don't like people to hurt you, so don't do it to others.

Brendan tries to ignore Fred's teasing.

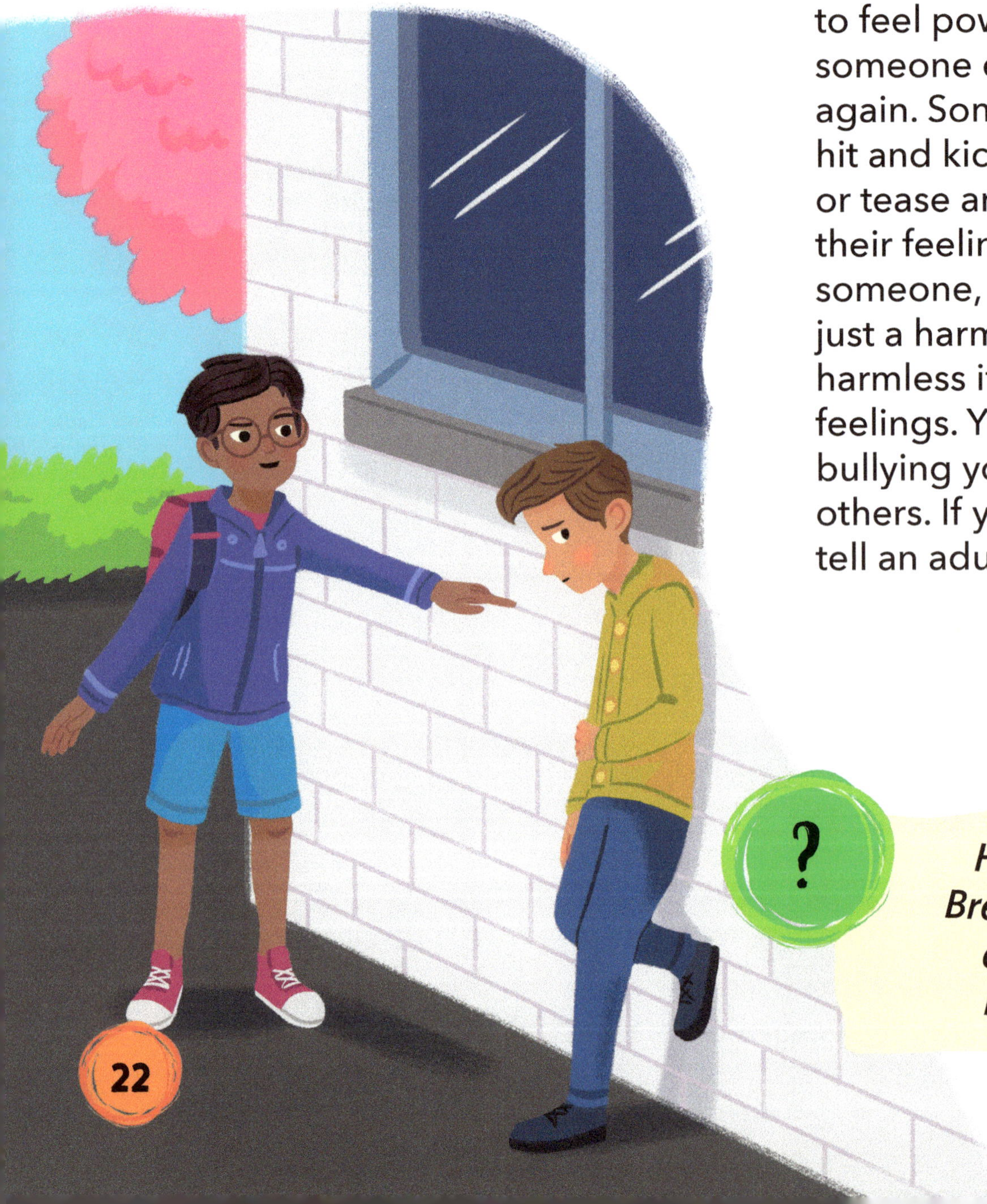

Bullying

A bully is someone who tries to feel powerful by picking on someone else over and over again. Sometimes a bully might hit and kick to hurt someone, or tease and make fun to hurt their feelings. If you tease someone, you might think it's just a harmless joke. But it's not harmless if you hurt someone's feelings. You don't like someone bullying you, so don't do it to others. If you are being bullied, tell an adult you trust.

?

How do you think Brendan feels? What can he do about Fred's bullying?

Right or Wrong?

Some people think that nasty behavior is okay as long as they don't get caught. For example, if you steal candy from the store or cheat on a spelling test and don't get caught, does that mean it's okay? The answer is a firm NO, it's not okay! You've still done something wrong and that kind of behavior is not honest or fair.

Amira goes to her teacher when she sees two other children fighting. Miss Kowalski will stop the fight and help the children sort out their differences.

?

Why should you tell a parent, teacher, or other adult if you see nasty behavior?

RESPECT

Respect is a word you have probably heard a lot. It means accepting someone for who they are. It doesn't matter whether people have lives like yours, or lives that are very different, you still need to respect them.

Stereotypes

Stereotypes are fixed ideas about people, or groups of people, that are often unfair. For instance, some fans of Football Team X may think that all Team Y fans are stupid. This is a negative and disrespectful way of thinking about a group of people. Stereotyping also happens when people sort all the people of a different skin color or religion into boxes that set them apart as different, often in a bad way.

When Laura visited Asha's house on Diwali, she helped make a rangoli pattern outside her door. Diwali is important to Asha's family and Laura respects that.

Respect For All

Learning to accept people regardless of their appearance, their family background, or their beliefs will lead to good, kind behavior. You can recognize people are different than you and respect those differences.

Think Positive!

Here are a few tips to help you believe in yourself and build self-respect:

- Focus on the good rather than the bad in your life.
- Make a list of the things you can do, such as read a book or ride a bike. Now make a list of the things you can't do YET but may be able to do in the future if you keep trying.
- Develop a growth mindset by thinking about yourself and your brain as something that changes and grows, rather than as something fixed. If you keep trying, you can improve your abilities and the way you think about yourself.

Lennox tries to imagine himself as a swimmer to help him get into the pool and remember what to do with his arms and legs.

YOU'RE IN CONTROL

Only you control how you behave. Think about the choices you make about your behavior. How will your behavior affect yourself and other people? How will it make you feel about yourself?

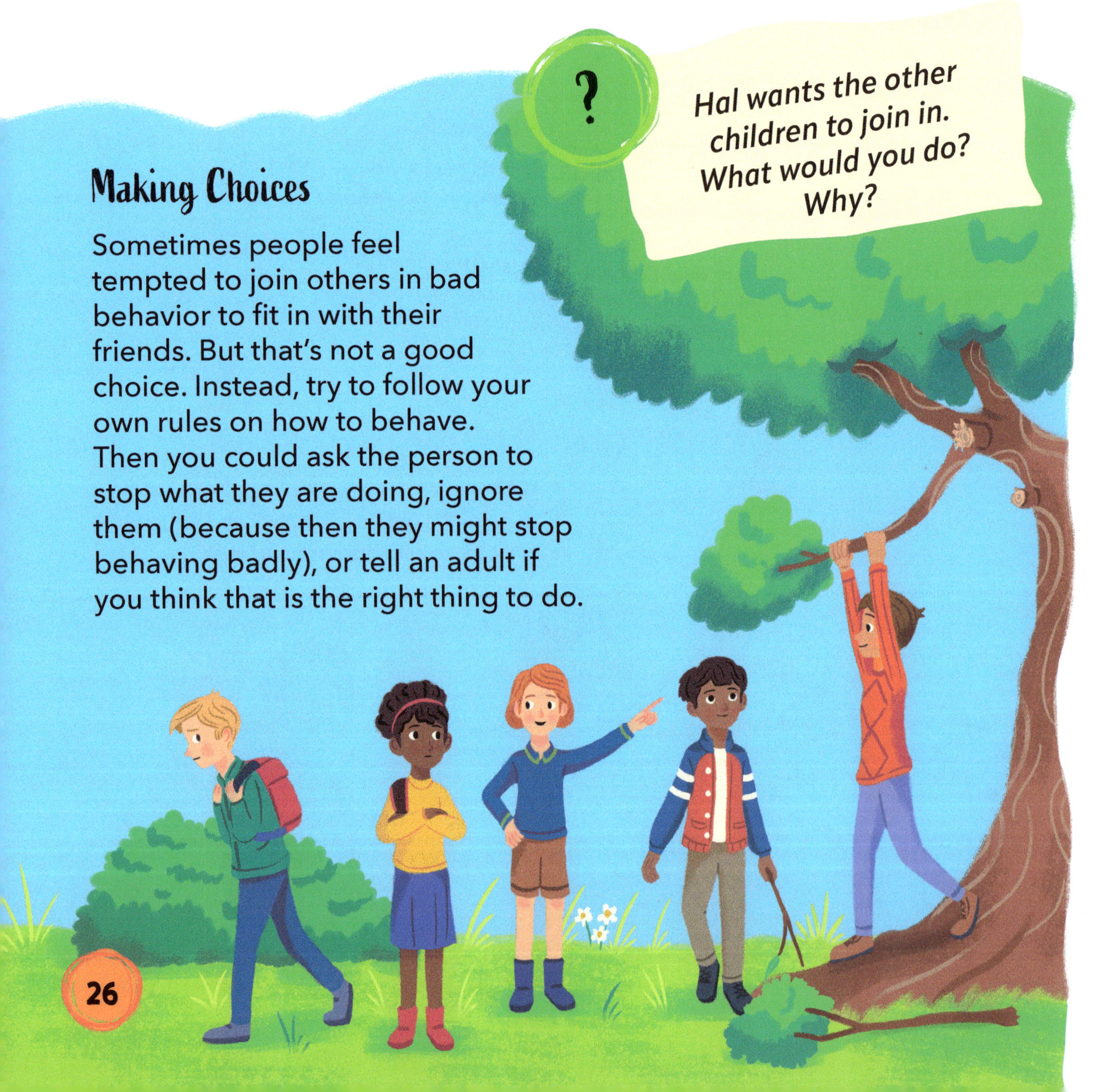

?

Hal wants the other children to join in. What would you do? Why?

Making Choices

Sometimes people feel tempted to join others in bad behavior to fit in with their friends. But that's not a good choice. Instead, try to follow your own rules on how to behave. Then you could ask the person to stop what they are doing, ignore them (because then they might stop behaving badly), or tell an adult if you think that is the right thing to do.

These children are behaving well on their camping trip. They are making the right choices and everyone is having a good time.

Think Before You Act

No one can behave their best every minute of the day, not even adults. But if you think before you act and treat other people the way you like to be treated, you're more likely to make the right choices about your behavior. You'll be happier, and so will everyone around you.

If you get your behavior wrong, say you're sorry and mean it. Then try to make a better choice next time.

THINGS TO TALK ABOUT AND DO

Before You Begin

Talk about behavior. How much can you control your own behavior? What ideas has this book given you to help you with your behavior?

Think and Talk

Respect
Talk about the importance of respecting people with different lives than your own. Return to pages 24–25 to remind yourself about this subject. If you are curious about other people's lives, it helps you understand and respect them more easily. What else might help you learn how to respect other people?

Write

Hopes and Dreams

Write a letter to your future self. Use this list of ideas to help you:

What job will you have?

How will you be helping the world or other people?

What challenges will you have overcome?

What will you have to work on to reach your dream job?

Who might help you along the way?

Create

Protect the Planet

Design a poster to encourage people to put litter in the garbage can or treat wild areas with more respect. Sketch out a few ideas on a piece of scrap paper. Use posterboard for your finished product.

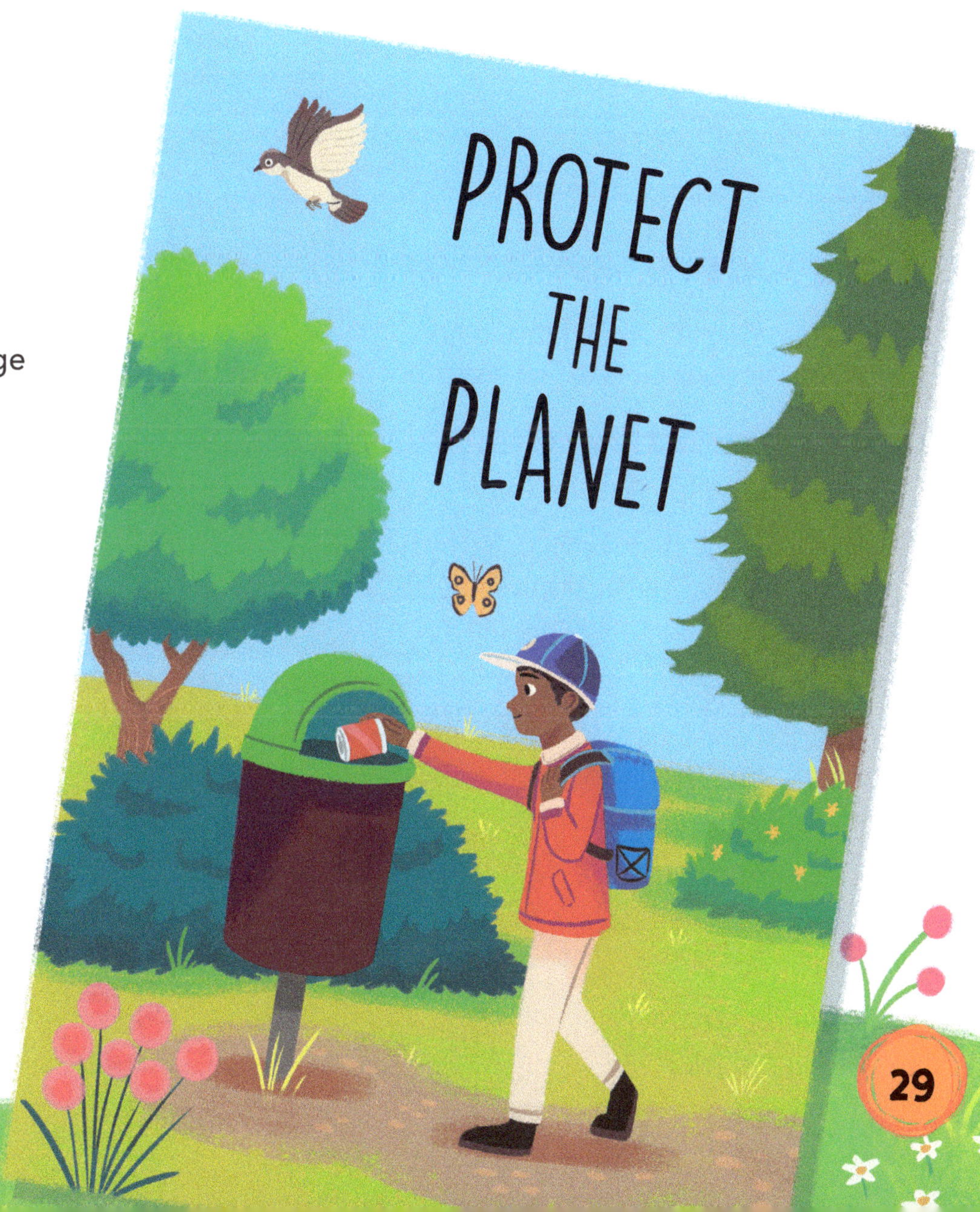

GLOSSARY

ability Being able to do something, such as read a book or jump over a jump rope.

appearance The way someone looks on the outside.

appreciate Be grateful for somebody or something.

argument Having an argument means not agreeing with someone else in a discussion and it can mean you get into a fight.

attention Taking notice of somebody or something. Paying attention means listening carefully.

behavior The way someone acts, or behaves, especially toward other people.

beliefs Strong feelings, or beliefs, that certain things are true or that somebody or something exists.

bullying Hurting or making fun of other people repeatedly in order to feel powerful.

chore A job that needs to be done, such as doing the dishes.

Diwali The festival of light celebrated by Hindus, Sikhs, and Jains in October or November each year. People celebrate by lighting candles and lamps, setting off fireworks, creating rangoli patterns, and gathering together.

emotion A strong feeling, such as love, fear, or happiness.

germ A small living thing that can cause infection or disease.

growth mindset Thinking about yourself and your brain as something that grows and changes, rather than as something that is fixed.

instructions Directions on what to do and how to do it.

interrupt Stopping somebody from speaking or doing something because you are wanting their attention.

manners Behaving in a polite way, being kind and helpful.

mood How a person is feeling.

nasty Hurtful behavior toward someone or something.

patient Willing to wait. It is polite to be patient.

polite Showing respect for other people, for example, using words such as "please" and "thank you."

recycle Turn a material into something else that can be used.

respect Accepting someone for who they are, whether they are like you or are very different.

rude Unkind or not showing respect for other people.

rule A statement, written down or said aloud, about what people must or must not do in a situation, such as when playing sports or driving a car on the road.

self-respect Feeling proud of yourself in what you do and say.

stereotype A fixed idea about people, or groups of people, that is often unfair.

table manners Polite ways of behaving when eating food with other people. They usually include using a knife, fork, or spoon rather than eating with your fingers.

TRUSTED ADULTS

Throughout this book, the author advises you to talk to a trusted adult if you are upset, afraid, or confused about something that is going on in your life. A trusted adult is someone you are happy to be around and who listens to what you say, or someone who has helped you before. It can be many people including your teacher, a teaching assistant, a nurse, your parents or caregivers, an older sibling, or your grandparents. Not all adults are trusted adults.

FURTHER INFORMATION

WEBSITES

Feelings
Your feelings affect your behavior. Learn more!
kidshealth.org/en/kids/feeling/

Kids Against Bullying
This site is a great resource if you're being bullied–or worry that you're the bully.
pacerkidsagainstbullying.org/

Stop Bullying
Find many links about this problem.
www.stopbullying.gov/

Talking About Your Feelings
Discover why discussing your emotions is healthy!
kidshealth.org/en/kids/talk-feelings.html

BOOKS

Bassier, Emma. *Manners All Around.* Minneapolis, MN: Cody Koala, 2020.

Brian, Rachel. *Consent (for Kids!): Boundaries, Respect, and Being in Charge of You.* New York, NY: Little, Brown and Company, 2020.

Martinez, Manuel. *What Is Respect? Giving Respect.* New York, NY: Rosen Classroom, 2020.

Miller, Marie-Therese. *Feeling Good About You.* North Mankato, MN: Rourke Educational Media, 2020.

Publisher's note to parents and teachers: Our editors have reviewed the websites listed here to make sure they're suitable for students. However, websites may change frequently. Please note that students should always be supervised when they access the internet.

INDEX